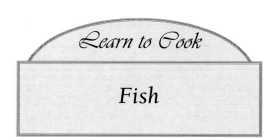

Learn to Cook

Fish

Learn to Cook

Fish

Janet Marsh Lillie

HARLAXTON

Page two: Trout with Almonds (p. 11). The secret of success for this succulent dish is to maintain an even heat and to keep the butter bubbling. The endpapers show the preparation for this classic dish.

Published by
Harlaxton Publishing Limited
2 Avenue Road, Grantham, Lincolnshire, NG31 6TA
United Kingdom
A Member of the Weldon International Group of Companies

First Published in 1994

© Copyright 1994 Harlaxton Publishing Limited
© Copyright 1994 Design Harlaxton Publishing Limited

Publisher: Robin Burgess
Project Coordinator: Barbara Beckett
Designer: Rachel Rush
Editor: Alison Leach
Illustrator: Maggie Renvoize
Jacket photographer: Rodney Weidland
Inside photography: Jack Sarafian
Food stylist: Janet Marsh Lillie
Produced by Barbara Beckett Publishing
Colour Separation: G.A. Graphics, Stamford, UK
Printer: Imago, Singapore

British Library Cataloguing-in-Publication data.
A catalogue record for this book is available from the British Library

Title: Learn to Cook, FISH
ISBN: 1 85837 082 5

Contents

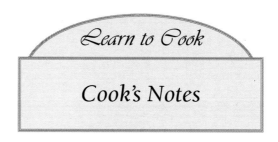

Cook's Notes

Measurements

All spoon and cup measurements are level. Standard spoon and cup measures are used in all the recipes. I recommend using a graduated nest of measuring cups: 1 cup, ½ cup, ⅓ cup and ¼ cup. The graduated nest of spoons comprises one tablespoon, 1 teaspoon, ½ teaspoon and ¼ teaspoon. For liquids, use a standard litre or imperial pint measuring jug which also shows cup measurements. As the metric/imperial/US equivalents given are not exact, follow only one system of measurement within each recipe.

Ovens should be preheated to the specified temperature. When cooking on the hob (stove plate), use medium heat where high, low or simmer are not specified.

Ingredients

Fresh fruit and vegetables should be used in the recipes unless otherwise stated. **Herb** quantities are for fresh herbs; if fresh are unobtainable, use half the quantity of dried herbs.Use freshly ground black **pepper** whenever pepper is listed; use **salt** and pepper to individual taste. Use plain (all-purpose) **flour** unless otherwise stated. Fresh **ginger** should be used throughout, unless ground ginger is called for. Use fresh **chillies**; if substituting dried chillies, halve the quantity. Cold-pressed virgin olive **oil** is recommended, but any type may be used. Use unsalted **butter**. Preferably use fermented wine **vinegar**; however, cider vinegar and malt vinegar may be substituted if preferred. White granulated **sugar** is used unless otherwise stated.

Cantonese Steamed Fish (p. 28). To bring out the delicate flavour of this elegant main course, retain the moisture by cooking the fish whole.

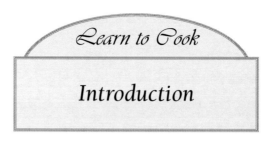

Introduction

When you learn to cook fish, a fantastic diversity of meals is added to your repertoire. The fish may be simply crumbed and pan- or shallow-fried in sizzling butter, dipped in a light batter and deep-fried until crispy and golden, marinated in garlic, ginger and lemon juice and steamed, poached in white wine and stock—even baked whole—every taste can be satisfied.

Nutritionally speaking, fish is an excellent source of protein and is low in calories (kilojoules) and cholesterol. It's easily digested and cooks quickly.

The instructions in this book are all clearly set out. There are step-by-step guides to the different cooking methods, such as poaching, braising and grilling (broiling). Sauces, tips and methods are cross-referenced within the book and there is also a glossary of cooking terms on page 47 so you can look up any term that is unfamiliar.

Be sure to read the information on measurements and ingredients on page 6 and also be aware of an important rule of cooking, which is always to read a recipe through before you start! Check you have all the ingredients called for, the equipment you need and enough time to complete the steps.

Fish cooking relies on a balance between dry goods you will no doubt already have in your cupboard and those familiar fresh produce items you often buy. Staples include flour, in plain (all-purpose), self-raising (self-rising) and cornflour (cornstarch) forms, eggs, caster (superfine) sugar, rice, potatoes, unsalted butter, nuts, seeds, and oil (including olive, peanut and hazelnut). A good stock of lemons is also essential, as is bread for making fresh crumbs.

Some of the more unusual products used in my recipes include tarragon vinegar, poppadums, couscous and curry paste. Aromatic and flavour-enhancing dry spices you'll need include cumin, cardamom, turmeric, oregano, chilli powder and bay leaves.

Handy equipment to have when cooking fish includes a good quality set of sharp knives

Gutting a Fish

Place the tip of the knife into the tiny hole below the tail and cut up towards the gills.	*Cut the gills from the backbone with the point of a sharp knife.*	*Take out the innards.*	*Scrape any further innards out and rinse under cold water.*

Filleting Fish

| Check fish for freshness. It should have bright eyes and firm flesh. | Make a cut behind the head and cut down to the backbone. | Turn the knife and cut carefully towards the tail. | Keep the knife close to the backbone. |

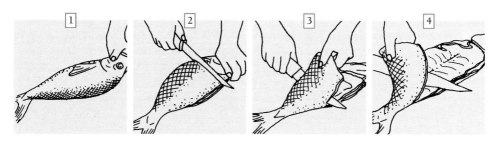

(for chopping, paring and filleting), a couple of frying pans (skillets) and saucepans with lids, a metal or bamboo steamer—even a cake rack can be used for steaming—and a wok is also a desirable utensil. Most other equipment mentioned in this book can be found in the average kitchen.

When a recipe refers to a **fatty** or **oily** fish, varieties fitting this description include tuna, salmon, and mackerel. **Lean** or **firm white** fish varieties include snapper, whiting, bream, trout, sole, flounder, cod, halibut, haddock and varieties of dory.

Enjoy cooking fish. It's so easy—and so tasty!

Preparation of Fish in Beer Batter (p. 18). A delicious contrast in textures results from this combination of crisp light coating with firm fish fillets.

Frying

Frying involves quick cooking in a small amount of fat, usually half butter and half oil, in a frying pan (skillet). The fish is usually added when the butter has melted and starts to foam. You should maintain a moderate temperature and only turn the fish once, very carefully. Cook only until fish is lightly browned and to the point when the flesh is beginning to flake from the bone. As a rule, the presentation side is always fried first. Remember also to dry the fish well before cooking to minimize spitting. It is usual to coat the fish with seasoned flour or a marinade before placing it in the hot pan. In the case of wok cooking or **stir-frying** (as in the Stir-Fried Fish Goujons with Cucumber recipe), the full amount of fat used is oil. Peanut oil is usually chosen because it can be heated to a very high temperature before it starts to smoke, at which point foods burns very quickly. **Shallow-frying** is a variation where just enough oil or a mixture of oil and butter is used to cover coated fish or simple fish cakes.

The fish selected for **deep-frying** should have a low fat content. Choose firm white fillets and dry them completely before coating and cooking. The pan should not be more than ½ to ¾ full of oil. Foods for deep-frying are usually coated in some sort of batter or textured coating. The purpose of this is to provide a golden crust, seal the fish and minimize absorption on immersion in the hot oil. When cooked, the fish should rise to the surface of the oil. Remove and drain immediately on paper towels and keep warm.

Preparation of Crunchy Coconut Fish (p. 16). An important step is to place the coated fish on a plate, cover and chill for 1 hour to set the coating before placing in the pan.

Trout with Almonds

Trout requires an even heat and bubbling butter if it is to cook perfectly. This versatile pan-fried dish can be served with a sprinkling of pepper and a wedge of lemon. This butter sauce with almond flakes is, however, both classic and popular.

4 x 250–300 g/9–11 oz trout, cleaned, head and
    tail left intact
2–3 tablespoons plain (all-purpose) flour for
    coating

125 g/4 oz/½ cup butter
Juice of 2 lemons
30 g/1 oz/2 tablespoons butter, extra
30 g/1 oz/¼

Pat the fish dry with paper towels. Put the flour into a polythene bag and season with salt and pepper. Add the trout to the bag and shake carefully.

Melt the 125 g/4 oz/½ cup butter in a frying pan (skillet), add half the lemon juice. When the butter starts to foam, add the flour-coated fish, cover the pan, reduce the heat to low and cook for 5 minutes on each side, or until the flesh is opaque and the skin is a rich, crisp brown.

Transfer each fish to a warmed serving dish and keep hot. Wipe the pan clean and melt the extra butter. Add the remaining lemon juice, almonds, salt and pepper and parsley, bring to the boil and pour over the fish. Serve immediately.

Serves 4

Storing Fish. *For general storage, scale and remove gills and guts if not already done, wash in cold water and dry well, wrap in clingfilm (plastic wrap) or foil and store in the refrigerator for up to 3 days. Freezing fish is not recommended because it loses some of its flavour on thawing. Never re-freeze fish.*

Frying Fish

| *Wash and dry the fish or fillets.* | *Melt the butter and oil in the pan.* | *Add the fish when butter is foaming.* | *Turn the fish once only.* |

Stir-Fried Fish Goujons with Cucumber

Cod, halibut or red snapper can be used here..

675 g/1½ lb firm white thick-cut fish fillets, cut
    into 5 x 2.5 cm/2 x 1 inch pieces
2 teaspoons salt
4 tablespoons soy sauce
3 tablespoons dry sherry
2 teaspoons cornflour (cornstarch)
3 tablespoons peanut oil
1 red pepper (capsicum, bell pepper), cut into
    diamonds or julienne strips

225 g/8 oz cucumber, peeled, sliced in half to
    remove seeds, cut to the size of the fish pieces
12 mangetout (snow peas), trimmed, cut in half
2 garlic cloves, crushed
2.5 cm/1 inch piece root ginger, cut into julienne
    strips
250 ml/8 fl oz/1 cup chicken stock
2 teaspoons cornflour (cornstarch), mixed to a
    paste with 1 tablespoon water
Cooked rice or fried noodles, to serve

Place the fish in a bowl containing a mixture of the salt, 2 tablespoons of the soy sauce, 1 table-spoon of the sherry and the cornflour. Leave to marinate for about 1 hour.

Heat a wok or large frying pan (skillet) and add 2 tablespoons of the peanut oil. Remove the fish pieces from the marinade (reserve) and add the fish pieces to the wok or pan. Stir-fry care-fully for about 2 minutes until lightly browned. Remove to paper towels to drain.

Reheat the wok or pan and add the remaining oil. When the oil is hot, add the pepper, cucum-ber, mangetout, garlic and ginger and stir-fry for 2 minutes. Add the remaining soy sauce and sherry and the chicken stock and cook for a further 3 minutes. Stir in the reserved marinade, return the fish pieces and cook gently until the fish is heated through. Serve with rice or noodles.
Serves 4

Chilli Fish Cakes

Any fish cake is popular–these rely on the fish being blended to a paste with seasonings, making it light and springy in texture. If red curry paste is not available, use a teaspoon of ground coriander.

450 g/1 lb firm white fish fillets, roughly chopped
2 teaspoons red curry paste
1 tablespoon light soy sauce
2–3 tablespoons cornflour (cornstarch)
1 egg, beaten

½–1 teaspoon finely chopped red chilli
2 tablespoons chopped spring onions (scallions)
60 g/2 oz/½ cup finely sliced French (green) beans
Oil for shallow-frying
Lime or lemon wedges, to serve

Stir-Fried Fish Goujons with Cucumber. A handy hint for this exotic fish dish is to work quickly over a high heat.

Crunchy Coconut Fish—a tropical delight that requires an egg and breadcrumb coating to ensure easy cooking.

Place the fish in a food processor. Process lightly until smooth. Add the curry paste, soy sauce, cornflour and egg. Process again until well combined. With a spatula, scrape the fish mixture into a bowl and stir in the red chilli, spring onions and beans. With oiled hands, take 3 table-spoons of the mixture at a time and shape into flat, round cakes.

Heat 2.5 cm/1 inch oil in a large frying pan (skillet). Place the cakes into the hot oil 3 at a time, and fry, shaking the pan gently to prevent sticking, until golden brown underneath. Turn the cakes over carefully, using an egg slice, and fry the other side until golden. Remove and drain on paper towels. Serve immediately with lemon or lime wedges or leave to cool.
Makes 6

Vinaigrette Dressing

3 tablespoons olive oil
2 tablespoons vinegar

1 teaspoon Dijon mustard
Salt and pepper

Combine all the ingredients in a small bowl, and whisk together to combine. Alternatively, place the ingredients in a screw-topped jar and shake vigorously to combine.
Makes about 90 ml/3 fl oz/⅓ cup

Crunchy Coconut Fish

8 x 60 g/2 oz firm white fish fillets such as Whiting
Plain (all-purpose) flour for coating

90 g/3 oz/1¾ cups desiccated (shredded) coconut
60 g/2 oz/¼

Roll the fish fillets in the flour, then dip each in the egg. Put the coconut in a polythene bag, add the fillets and shake to coat. Place on a plate, cover and chill for at least 1 hour. This sets the coating and makes the fish easier to cook.

Melt the butter and heat the oil in a large frying pan (skillet). When foaming subsides, add fish fillets and fry until the crust is golden, turning once.
Serves 4

Parmesan Coating. In place of the coconut, a mixture of equal quantities of dried breadcrumbs and grated Parmesan cheese makes an interesting variation.

Fish Grenobloise

Tiny tangy lemon wedges and capers create a quick brown-butter sauce for this interesting pan-fried fish.

175 g/6 oz/¾ cup butter
6 x 200 g/7 oz firm white fish fillets
4 tablespoons plain (all-purpose) flour for coating
60 g/2 oz/ ¼

2 lemons, peeled, pith removed and flesh chopped
finely
1 tablespoon chopped parsley

Melt the butter in a frying pan (skillet) over a moderate heat. Pat the fish dry with paper towels, place in a polythene bag with the flour and toss gently to coat. Shake the excess flour from the fish and place in the pan with the butter. Cook, turning once only with an egg slice, until the fish is golden brown and flakes easily. Remove the fish from the pan and keep warm. Add the capers and lemon to the pan and stir to heat through. Place the fish on a serving plate, and sprinkle with the parsley. Season the sauce with salt and pepper and pour over the fish. Serve immediately.
Serves 6

Spicy Blackened Fish

Cajun-creole in style, these fish fillets are coated with a herb and spice marinade, then carefully fried. They are delicious served with an avocado, melon and lettuce salad.

30 g/1 oz/½ cup chopped fresh coriander (cilantro)	2 tablespoons lemon juice
4 garlic cloves, crushed	½ teaspoon black pepper
1 tablespoon paprika	6 x 200 g/7 oz firm white fish fillets
¼ teaspoon cayenne pepper	Oil for shallow-frying
125 ml/4 fl oz/½ cup olive oil	Lime or lemon wedges

Mix the coriander, garlic, paprika, cayenne pepper, olive oil, lemon juice and pepper together in a bowl. Place the fish fillets in a dish and brush liberally with the marinade. Cover and chill overnight. Heat about 2.5 cm/1 inch oil in a frying pan (skillet), and then add the fish in batches. Cook for 2-3 minutes on each side, turning once only, until crisp and lightly browned. Remove and drain on paper towels. Serve immediately with lime or lemon wedges.

Serves 4

Crunchy Almond Fish

Thick fillets of fish are easy to cut into strips (called goujons) for this summer-style recipe. Serve the accompanying salad well chilled so the hot crunchy fish will provide a delicious contrast with the cool green leaves.

150–200 g/5–7 oz firm white fish fillets	125 g/4 oz mangetout (snow peas) or French
3 tablespoons cornflour (cornstarch)	(green) beans, blanched (p. 31)
Salt and pepper	1 red pepper (capsicum, bell pepper), cut into
3 egg whites, lightly beaten	julienne strips
200 g/7 oz/2 cups unblanched almonds, chopped	Oil and vinegar dressing (vinaigrette) (p. 14)
Oil for shallow-frying	Easy Tartare Sauce, to serve (p. 17)
200 g/7 oz mixed small lettuce leaves	

Cut the fish fillets into 24 strips. Place in a polythene bag, add the cornflour, season with salt and pepper. Shake to coat the fish thoroughly, then remove from the bag. Dip in the egg white, then in the almonds, pressing them on firmly.

Heat about 2.5 cm/1 inch oil in a large frying pan (skillet). Fry the fish strips in batches until golden. Drain on paper towels. Keep hot.

Toss the lettuce, vegetables and dressing together in a bowl. Arrange the goujons on top and serve with tartare or soured cream sauce.

Serves 4–6

Fresh Breadcrumbs. *Cut the crusts from a few slices of day-old bread. Place the bread in a food processor or blender and 'pulse' (turn machine on and off every second or two), to obtain roughly chopped crumbs.*

Easy Tartare Sauce

250 ml/8 floz/1 cup soured cream
1 tablespoon snipped chives
1 tablespoon chopped dill

2 finely chopped gherkins
1 teaspoon capers

Combine all the ingredients in a bowl; chill and serve.
Makes about 250 ml/8 fl oz/1 cup

Potato Chips (French Fries)

500 g/18 oz potatoes   *Oil for frying*

Peel and remove the 'eyes' or holes from the potatoes. Cover with water while you are preparing them to avoid browning. For straight-edged chips, trim the potatoes to straighten the sides. Cut them evenly in to the desired thickness: for French fries, 1 x 1 x 6 cm/½ x ½ x 2½ inches; for matchsticks/shoestrings, 6 mm x 6 mm x 5 cm (¼ x ¼ x 2 inches). Alternatively, slice into thick 'wedges' or paper-thin wafers. Wash the chips under running water to allow some of the starch to escape. Dry well to prevent spitting when frying.

Heat about 7.5 cm/3 inches oil in a large saucepan or wok until it is hot. (The oil is too hot if it starts smoking and rippling on the surface.) Lower the chips into the oil in batches and cook for 5–7 minutes or until golden brown and floating to the top of the oil. Remove with a slotted spoon. Drain on paper towels.
Serves 4–6

Deep-Frying Fish

| *Coat the fish fillets in flour, yoghurt and then breadcrumbs.* | *Heat the oil in a large saucepan no more than ⅔ full.* | *Cook fish until golden and lift out with a slotted spatula.* | *Drain off fat on paper towels.* |

Toasting Nuts and Sesame Seeds. *Spread the nuts or seeds on a baking sheet. Bake in a preheated oven at 180°C/350°F/gas 4 for 4 minutes, remove from the oven, shake the tray or turn the nuts over with a fork. Bake a further 3–4 minutes or until golden. Remove the nuts from the hot tray immediately, or they will continue to cook. Avoid using black baking sheets. Alternatively, dry-fry the nuts by placing them in a frying pan (skillet) over a low to moderate heat for 2–4 minutes, shaking the pan to turn the nuts so that they colour evenly. Pine nuts cook very quickly, so be careful!*

Honey Sesame Fish

Plain yoghurt replaces beaten egg for the coating here. When deep-frying, the amount of oil required will depend on the size of the saucepan or deep-fryer. It is important, however, that the food be completely immersed in the hot oil for the fish to cook quickly and evenly.

2 tablespoons sesame seeds, toasted (above)
90 g/3 oz/1½ cups day-old fresh breadcrumbs (p. 17)
675 g/1½ lb firm white fish fillets, cut into 4 cm/ 1½ inch portions

Plain (all-purpose) flour, seasoned with salt and pepper
400 ml/14 fl oz/1¾ cups plain yoghurt
Vegetable oil for frying
1 tablespoon clear honey

Combine the sesame seeds with the breadcrumbs in a bowl. Coat the fish portions in the seasoned flour, dip in the yoghurt and press the sesame-breadcrumb mixture firmly on to the fish portions.

Heat the oil in a large saucepan. When a cube of bread dropped into it turns golden in about 30 seconds or the oil reaches 130°C/350°F on a thermometer, add the fish, and cook for 4–5 minutes or until the fish is crisp and golden. Lift out with a slotted spoon and drain on paper towels. Combine the remaining yoghurt with the honey. Serve with the fish.

Serves 4

Fish in Beer Batter

A batter prepared with beer makes a very light, crisp coating for any firm white fish fillets such as whiting, grouper or sea bass. A wedge of lemon, a sprinkling of vinegar or tartare sauce and crisp chips are all you need for a scrumptious meal. The fish tastes even better if it is served wrapped in newspaper or butcher's paper.

200 g/7 oz/1¾ cups self-raising (self-rising) flour
½ teaspoon paprika
Salt and pepper
250 ml/8 fl oz/1 cup beer
125 ml/4 fl oz/½ cup water

Vegetable oil for frying
3 tablespoons plain (all-purpose) flour
6 x 200 g/7 oz firm white fish fillets, each cut in half
Potato chips, to serve (p. 17)
Lemon wedges or vinegar, to serve

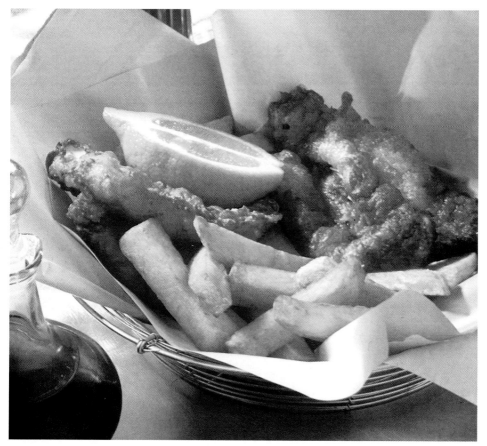

Fish in Beer Batter. The additional tart taste of lemon, vinegar or tartare sauce highlights this delicious meal.

Sift the flour, paprika, salt and pepper into a large bowl and make a well in the centre. Pour in the beer and water and whisk together to make a smooth batter. Allow to stand 1 hour if time permits, so that the batter thickens slightly.

Heat enough oil in a deep-fryer, saucepan or wok to cover the fish portions. When a cube of bread turns golden in about 30 seconds, or the oil reaches 180°C/350°F on a thermometer, it is ready.

Dry the fish portions with paper towels to minimize spitting while frying. Coat four to six fish fillets lightly in the plain flour and dip in the beer batter. Drain the excess on to the rim of the bowl before carefully lowering into the hot oil. Cook for 5–6 minutes or until golden brown. Lift from the oil on to paper towels and leave to drain in a warm oven. Repeat this procedure until all the fillets are cooked. Serve immediately with potato chips (p. 17) and lemon wedges or vinegar.
Serves 4

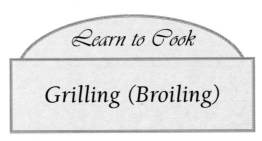

Grilling (Broiling)

Grilling (broiling) or barbecuing cooks fish very quickly because of the high direct heat involved. These cooking methods are suitable for all types of fish, but particularly for those with a high oil content, such as tuna and salmon. If using whole fish, remember to slash the skin slightly to allow the heat to penetrate. Allow 4 minutes for each 200 g/7 oz and turn only once during that period. For fillets, steaks and cutlets allow 10–12 minutes, again turning only once. The grill pan (broiler) is often greased or lined with foil to prevent sticking. Frequent basting of the fish is essential. Remember that the fish will continue to cook for a few minutes after removal from the heat.

Salmon Steaks with Lemon Parsley Butter

Lemon parsley butter is the simplest sauce you can make to serve with any grilled (broiled) fish–butter mixed with chopped capers, cracked black pepper, snipped chives or dill are alternative flavourings.

4 x 200 g/7 oz salmon steaks
Salt and pepper
60 g/2 oz/¼ cup butter, melted
125 g/4 oz/½ cup extra butter, softened

2 tablespoons finely chopped parsley
2 tablespoons lemon juice
Salt and pepper
Small boiled potatoes, to serve

Season both sides of the salmon steaks with salt and pepper. Place the steaks on a greased grill pan (broiler). Brush the salmon with melted butter and grill (broil) for 3–5 minutes on each side or until cooked (p. 23). Beat the extra butter and parsley together in a bowl until creamy and smooth. Beat in the lemon juice and season with salt and pepper. Serve the salmon steaks and potatoes with the lemon parsley butter.
Serves 4

Bacon Fish Brochettes

Skewer cooking is very popular and easy to prepare in advance. When using wooden skewers, make sure they are soaked in water for 30 minutes or longer before use to prevent them burning when the brochettes are cooked. For this recipe you will need eight 15 cm/6 inch skewers.

Grilling (Broiling) Fish

| Make shallow slashes in the skin to allow heat to penetrate. | Brush the fish with melted butter, salt and pepper. | Put on a greased grill pan (broiler). | Turn once. |

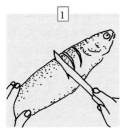  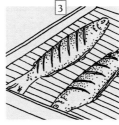 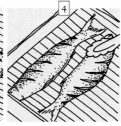

4 x 125 g/4 oz thick firm white fish fillets, each cut into 6 pieces
8 rashers (slices) bacon, rinds removed, each cut into 3 strips

Hollandaise sauce (p. 21)
Oil for basting

Wrap each piece of fish around a strip of bacon and thread three on to each wooden skewer. Place on a grill pan (broiler). Brush the brochettes with a little oil, cook under a preheated grill (broiler), turning once or twice, for 5–10 minutes or until the fish is white in colour and bacon is cooked and slightly crisp. Serve with Hollandaise sauce.
Serves 4

Hollandaise Sauce

4 tablespoons vinegar
5 teaspoons water
12 peppercorns
3 egg yolks

300 g/11 oz/1⅓ cups butter
Juice of 1 lemon
Salt and pepper

Place the vinegar, water and peppercorns in a pan and boil to reduce to a third of its original volume. Allow to cool. Add the yolks and whisk over a gentle heat until creamy. Melt the butter and allow the sediment to settle. Remove the yolk mixture from the heat and whisk in the butter gradually. Add the lemon juice and season with salt and pepper.
Makes about 475 ml/¾ pint/2 cups

Preparation of Fresh Herbs. *Fresh herbs have a tendency to bruise and darken in colour when cut. To avoid this, tear roughly instead.*

Garlic Tuna with Chilli Tomatoes

This robust tomato, pepper and chilli combination, which is Spanish in style, is an ideal sauce for firm oily fish like tuna.

125 ml/4 fl oz/½ cup olive oil

2 onions, sliced

2 small green chillies, seeds removed, finely sliced

3 red peppers (capsicums, bell peppers), cut into
    julienne strips

1 kg/2¼ lb tomatoes, peeled (p. 45), cut into dice

Salt and pepper

3 tablespoons red wine vinegar

4 x 150 g/5 oz tuna steaks

1–2 tablespoons olive oil

Pepper

SAUCE

2 tablespoons olive oil

2 large garlic cloves, finely chopped

Heat the 125 ml/4 fl oz/½ cup olive oil in a saucepan. Add the onions and cook over a gentle heat for about 5 minutes, or until the onions soften. Add the chillies and red peppers and cook for a further 10 minutes. Add the tomatoes, and cook for another 10 minutes. Season with salt and pepper and leave to stand.

To make the sauce, heat the 2 tablespoons of olive oil in a separate pan and add the garlic. Fry gently for about 3 minutes until golden. Add the red wine vinegar to 'deglaze' the pan, scraping the bottom of the pan to lift any garlic pieces that may have stuck.

Meanwhile, brush each tuna steak with some of the extra olive oil and season with pepper. Place the steaks under a preheated grill (broiler) and cook for 3–5 minutes on each side, or until still a little pink in the centre. Spoon the chilli tomatoes into the centre of each plate, top with the grilled tuna steaks and the combined garlic cloves and olive oil sauce .

Serves 4

Garlic Tuna with Chilli Tomatoes. The hot and saucy combination of tomato, pepper and chilli sets off the tuna steaks perfectly. To prepare (left) Garlic Tuna with Chilli Tomatoes, place the tuna steaks under a preheated grill (broiler) and cook until a little pink in the centre.
Overleaf: Cantonese Steamed Fish (left)(p. 28), Garlic Tuna with Chilli Tomatoes (right) (left) and Basque Fish Pie (p. 43)—an international trio, offering a variety of exciting and distinctive flavours.

When Is It Cooked? *Fish is cooked when the flesh is opaque (white/cloudy) in colour, the juices run clear and the flesh flakes easily when a fork or tip of a knife is inserted into the thickest section or near the bone. Whole fish, on the other hand, will feel firm to touch and it will continue to cook for a few minutes after being removed from the heat.*

Banana Fish in a Parcel

2 garlic cloves, crushed

1 teaspoon caster (superfine) sugar

2 small red or green chillies, seeds removed and
    finely chopped

125 ml/4 fl oz/½ cup soy sauce

3 tablespoons lemon juice

4 x 150 g/5 oz whole firm white fish, cleaned and
    scaled

2 bananas, peeled, skins reserved

2 lemons, thinly sliced

Combine the garlic, sugar, chillies, soy sauce and lemon juice in a bowl. Add the fish and marinate for 30 minutes. Drain and place each fish on a square of foil. Reserve the marinade.

Mash the bananas in a bowl. Place some mashed banana and 1 tablespoon of the marinade over each fish and cover with lemon slices and some banana skin. Wrap completely in the foil. Cook under a preheated hot grill (broiler) for 10 minutes on each side. Place the marinade in a pan and simmer for 3 minutes, adding more sugar and water if necessary. Open the fish parcels, remove the banana skins, pour on some hot marinade and serve.

Serves 4

Whiting with Scallops and Caviar

Plain yoghurt is an excellent marinade base for these skewered, rolled, scallop-stuffed fish fillets which, once grilled (broiled), are served with a caviar yoghurt sauce made from the marinade.

500 g/18 oz whiting or other firm white fish fillets,
    cut into 12 pieces

12 scallops

200 ml/7 fl oz/¾ cup plain yoghurt

1 tablespoon chopped parsley

1 tablespoon snipped chives

2 spring onions (scallions), finely chopped

1 tablespoon lemon juice

Salt and pepper

30 g/1 oz/2 tablespoons butter

30 g/1 oz red lumpfish caviar

Watercress or dill, to serve

Place a scallop at the end of each whiting fillet and roll up with the scallop coral showing at the side. Secure with a wooden cocktail stick (toothpick). Place in a shallow dish.

Combine the yoghurt, parsley, chives, spring onions and lemon juice. Season lightly with salt and pepper. Spoon over the whiting rolls and marinate for 1–2 hours.

Remove the whiting rolls from the marinade, shake off the excess. Place the rolls in a shallow heatproof dish. Top each with a little piece of butter. Cook under a preheated grill (broiler) for 8–10 minutes, or until the fillets are cooked (p. 23). Remove the cocktail sticks carefully.

Stir half the caviar into the remaining marinade to make a sauce. Spoon a little caviar sauce on to plates and place three whiting rolls on top. Garnish with the remaining caviar and watercress or dill.

Serves 4

Steaming

This method is appropriate for most cuts of fish, particularly those that are firm and white, unlike their oily-natured relatives. The fish is placed in either a bamboo or metal perforated steamer, or for a more modern makeshift approach, a cake rack placed over a wok half-filled with water. As with poaching, the water is kept at simmering point. The fish is always covered, and may be seasoned with a selection of spices. This method is relied upon extensively in Oriental countries.

For whole fish, allow 8–12 minutes for each 200 g/7 oz from the time the water starts simmering. For fillets, steak and cutlets, allow 8–12 minutes.

Steaming Fish

Make shallow slashes on both sides of the fish.	*Put on a heatproof plate and garnish.*	*Put in the steamer and cook, covered, for 20 minutes.*	*Pour sauce over the fish. Garnish.*
1	2	3	4

Preparation of Cantonese Steamed Fish (p. 28) Place a rack in a wok, fish kettle or other deep pan.

Cantonese Steamed Fish

2 x 1 kg/2¼ lb whole firm white fish
1 teaspoon salt
5 cm/2 inch piece root ginger, peeled, cut into
    thin slices

2 tablespoons soy sauce
8 spring onions (scallions), finely sliced
4 tablespoons peanut oil
Cooked rice, to serve

Make three or four shallow slashes on each side of the fish. Rub the fish on both sides with the salt and leave to stand for 20 minutes. Place fish on a heatproof platter. Scatter the sliced ginger over the top.

Place a wire or bamboo rack into a wok, fish kettle or other deep pan. Fill with about 5 cm/ 2 inches of hot water. Bring the water to a simmer. Place the platter holding the fish on to the rack. Cover the wok, fish kettle or pan tightly and steam gently over a medium heat for 20 minutes.

Remove the platter and cooked fish and pour off all the liquid from the platter. Pour the soy sauce over the fish and scatter the spring onions over and around. Heat the oil in a pan until it just smokes, pour this over the fish and serve at once with rice.

Serves 4

Salmon with Roasted Hazelnuts

Salmon fillets are superb when steamed. They will only take a short time to cook. Don't allow the fish to become overcooked–a slightly pink centre is perfect. Serve with hazelnut vinaigrette and steamed potatoes amd steamed potatoes.

150 g/5 oz/1¼ cups hazelnuts

HAZELNUT DRESSING
125 ml/4 fl oz/½ cup hazelnut oil
Juice of ¼ lemon
Salt and pepper

2 x 500 g/18 oz whole salmon fillets, cut through
    on an angle into 2 portions
2 courgettes (baby marrows, zucchini), cut into
    fine julienne strips
½ bunch chives, snipped
Small steamed potatoes, to serve

Roast the hazelnuts in a preheated oven at 200°C/400°F/Gas 8 for 10–15 minutes or until the skins are toasted. Cool and rub off the skins. Chop the hazelnuts finely.

To make the dressing, whisk the hazelnut oil, lemon juice, salt and pepper together in a bowl.

Using a bamboo or metal steamer or a cake rack in a wok or deep pan, arrange salmon fillets, skinned side down, and top with the courgettes. Add about 5 cm/2 inch water. Steam for about 5 minutes or until the fish is sealed on the outside but still a little pink in the centre. Remove, using an egg slice.

Place each fillet on a warmed serving plate. Spoon over 2 tablespoons of the hazelnut dressing and scatter over the chopped hazelnuts and snipped chives. Serve immediately.

Serves 4

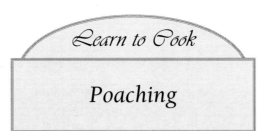
Poaching

This method of cooking is particularly suitable for whole fish or smaller cuts. The fish and the flavouring ingredients are placed in a pan and covered with water which is then brought to the boil. The pan is either removed from the heat or held at simmering point for a short period. A court bouillon is commonly used for poaching fish. It consists of water, wine or vinegar, roughly chopped vegetables, such as onion, carrot and celery, herbs and peppercorns. This poaching liquid can subsequently be reserved as the basis for an accompanying sauce.

Lemon Ginger Turbans

½ *red pepper (capsicum, bell pepper), cut into*
   julienne strips
1 carrot, cut into julienne strips
2 celery sticks, cut into julienne strips
8 x 60 g/2 oz firm white fish fillets, skins removed
250 ml/8 fl oz/1 cup water
3 tablespoons dry white wine
1 thyme sprig

1 bay leaf
5 peppercorns
2 tablespoons clear honey
3 tablespoons lemon juice
2 tablespoons sherry
1 garlic clove, crushed
12 mm/½ inch piece fresh root ginger, grated
Steamed rice, to serve

Preparation of Fish in Caper Butter Sauce (p. 31). The subtly piquant sauce complements these delicious fish steaks perfectly.

Fish in Caper Butter Sauce.

Combine the julienne vegetables and place some on the tail end of each fillet. Roll up and secure with wooden cocktail sticks (toothpicks).

Put the water, wine, thyme, bay leaf and peppercorns in a large frying pan (skillet). Place the fish rolls in the liquid and poach for about 3 minutes, or until they are white in colour throughout. Drain the fish on paper towels and transfer to a warmed serving dish.

Place the honey, lemon juice, sherry, garlic and ginger in a small saucepan and stir continuously until the sauce thickens slightly. Remove the wooden cocktail sticks from the fish and serve with the sauce. Accompany with steamed rice.

Serves 4

Blanching Vegetables. *Bring a large saucepan of water to the boil. Cut vegetables into the desired shape (florets, if broccoli or cauliflower, or if celery, carrot or courgette, into sticks of about 9 mm x 9 mm x 7.5 cm (⅜ x ⅜ x 3 inches). Put the vegetables into a strainer or colander that will fit into your saucepan. Plunge the vegetables into boiling water for about 20 seconds, drain and plunge immediately into iced water to arrest further cooking so the vegetables will retain their crispness. Drain and use as required. This process is used to soften vegetables slightly and bring out their colour.*

Fish in Caper Butter Sauce

2 brown onions, finely sliced
4 sprigs thyme
1 unpeeled garlic clove, crushed
1 teaspoon salt
¼ teaspoon pepper
1 lemon, cut into slices
4 x 200 g/7 oz thick, firm, white fish steaks

1 litre/1¾ pints/4¼ cups water
125 ml/4 fl oz/½ cup tarragon or wine vinegar
125 g/4 oz/½ cup butter, cut into small pieces
2 tablespoons capers, finely chopped
1 wedge cabbage, central core removed, finely
   sliced, blanched (above), to serve
1 leek, cut into ribbons, blanched (above), to serve

Combine the onions, thyme, garlic, salt, pepper and lemon slices in a pan. Add the fish and cover with water. Cover and bring to simmering point, remove from the heat. Reserve 250 ml/ 8 fl oz/1 cup of the liquid and leave the fish to stand in the remaining liquid for about 10 minutes.

Place the reserved liquid in a saucepan, cook over a high heat for about 5 minutes until reduced by half. Add the tarragon or wine vinegar and boil for about 1 minute. Reduce the heat to low and whisk in the butter gradually, ensuring each piece is mixed in before adding more. Add the capers and season with salt and pepper.

Remove the fish from the pan. Place the blanched cabbage and leek on warm serving plates, top with the fish, and pour over the sauce.
Serves 4

Poaching Fish

| *Put the wine, herbs and pepper into a pan.* | *Place the fish in the pan and cover with water.* | *Cover the pan and bring to the boil. Remove from heat.* | *Leave fish to stand in the liquid for 10 minutes to finish cooking.* |

Baking

This method of cooking is suitable for all cuts of fish—both whole and portions. Because fish flesh is so delicate and lean, it is recommended that oil or melted butter be brushed over regularly during the cooking process to protect the fish from drying out. Rapid cooking by this method helps to keep particularly lean fish moist. Some of the following recipes have either liquid or a topping poured over them for added protection. Always preheat your oven to a moderate temperature (180°C/350°F/gas 4, as a guide) for best results. For whole fish, allow 10 minutes for each 200 g/7 oz. For fillets or steaks, 20–30 minutes.

The foil baking method is an excellent way of retaining flavour and moisture. The physical barrier reduces greatly the evaporation of juices and in effect serves as a steaming implement. The fish is placed on a section of foil large enough to enclose the fish. It is seasoned and topped with vegetables or herbs, nuts and fruit, or even seafood, as you will see in the following recipes. The foil is gathered around the fish and its accompaniments, sealed tightly into an 'envelope' and baked in the oven for a designated time, which is usually only up to 10 minutes.

Tomato-Lemon Fish

Select firm fish fillets or cutlets for this dish. Serve with steamed potatoes or rice and a salad.

1 lemon, cut into 8 thin slices
4 x 200 g/7 oz firm white fish fillets or cutlets
2 tomatoes, each cut into 4 slices
2 courgettes (baby marrows, zucchini), thinly sliced

Pepper
A few sprigs Italian (flat leafed) parsley or basil
leaves

Cut four matching squares of foil and place two lemon slices in the centre of each. Place a fish fillet or cutlet on top, add two slices of tomato and some slices of courgette, season with pepper and top with parsley or basil leaves. Fold over the foil to seal the fish into tight parcels. Place on a hot barbecue/grill (broiler) for 4–10 minutes depending on their thickness, or bake in a preheated oven at 180°C/350°F/gas 4 for 6–10 minutes.
Serves 4

Tomato-Lemon Fish. You would be forgiven for thinking this dish had Mediterranean origins—perhaps it's the Italian parsley!

Variations. Ingredients are listed in the order in which they are placed on the foil:

Sliced tomatoes, breadcrumbs, a little curry powder, sultanas, fish, pepper, a little dry white wine.

Olive oil and a little lemon juice or sherry brushed on to both sides of fish.

Very thinly sliced mushrooms, thin strips of celery and carrot, fish, lemon juice or white wine.

Very thinly sliced leeks, fish, more leeks and a little dry white wine.

Foil Baking or En Papillote

Cut a foil square large enough to contain each fish.   *Place seasoning vegetables in centre of foil.*   *Place fish fillet on top with herbs and lemon slices.*   *Fold the foil over to seal the fish in secure parcels.*

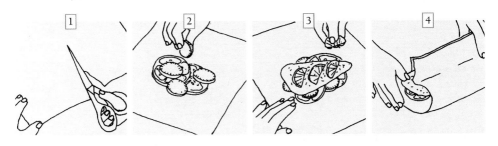

Preparation of Tomato-Lemon Fish (p. 32). Foil is used in this dish to protect the fish during cooking and to retain the moisture and delicious flavour.

Cleaning Leeks. *Cut off and discard any dark green leaves. They're too tough and can be bitter. If using as a whole vegetable, cut down the middle of the leek to about 2.5 cm/1 inch of the root end. Wash thoroughly under cold water, spreading the layers gently, making sure all the grit is washed out. Slice or chop as required.*

Seafood Snapper in Foil

If prawns (shrimp) and scallops are not available, substitute thin strips of blanched celery, carrot and leek.

2 leeks, cut into thin slices and blanched (above)
4 x 200 g/7 oz snapper fillets
12 scallops
8 large green prawns (shrimp), peeled and cleaned
2.5 cm/1 inch piece root ginger, cut into julienne
    strips

1 teaspoon lemon peel
4 teaspoons lemon juice
60 g/2 oz/¼ cup butter, melted
Salt and pepper

Cut foil into four 30 cm/12 inch diameter circles. Place blanched leeks in the centre of each foil circle and lay a fish fillet on top. Arrange the scallops and prawns on top and sprinkle with the ginger and lemon peel. Spoon over the lemon juice and butter. Season with salt and pepper.

Gather up the edges of foil and fold over to seal the parcels. Place on a baking sheet and bake in a preheated oven at 200°C/400°F/gas 6 for 10–12 minutes, or until cooked (p. 23).

Place each fish parcel on an individual plate. Fold back the edges of the foil and serve at once or slide the contents of the parcel on to the plate.

Serves 4

Date and Almond Baked Fish

This unusual stuffing mixture adds a Middle Eastern flavour to whole fish. Wrapped in foil, this dish can be prepared in advance.

250 g/9 oz/1¾ cups roughly chopped dates
125 g/4 oz/1 cup ground blanched almonds
3 tablespoons butter, melted
½ teaspoon ground cinnamon
1 tablespoon chopped coriander (cilantro)
2.5 cm/1 inch piece root ginger, finely chopped

5 tablespoons lemon juice
Pepper
6 x 350–425 g/12–15 oz whole firm white fish,
    cleaned and scaled (p. 36)
Oil for brushing
Cooked rice or couscous, to serve

Combine the dates, almonds, butter, cinnamon, coriander, ginger and lemon juice in a bowl, season with pepper. Mix well.

Pat the fish dry with paper towels. Cut six sheets of foil large enough to wrap each fish completely. Brush with oil. Divide the date mixture between the sheets of foil, place the fish on top and sprinkle over any remaining mixture.

Wrap the foil tightly around the fish and bake in a preheated oven at 180°C/350°/gas 4 for 20 minutes, or until cooked (p. 23). Cut open the foil, serve with cooked rice or couscous.

Serves 6

Scaling Fish. To scale, hold the fish by the tail and scrape with a knife from the tail to the head. Repeat with the other side of the backbone over a large sheet of paper. Remove any fins with a sharp pair of scissors, being careful as they may be quite spiky.

Baking a Whole Fish

| *Place fish in a baking dish and pour over wine and melted butter.* | *Sprinkle on spring onions (scallions) and carrot. Cover with foil. Bake for 15 minutes.* | *Remove from oven. Pour pan juices into a saucepan to make sauce.* | *Place fish on a warm plate and serve the sauce separately.* |

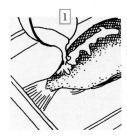 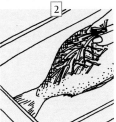  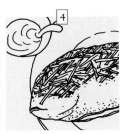

Snapper Calabrese

Olives and capers in this tomato sauce add a robust Italian flavour to any baked firm, white whole fish.

4 x 350–450 g/17 oz–1 lb whole snapper, scaled (above)
Salt and pepper
1 lemon, thinly sliced
90 g/3 oz/6 tablespoons butter
3 tablespoons capers, drained
10 black olives or stuffed olives, sliced

1 tablespoon oregano leaves
400 g/14 oz canned peeled tomatoes or fresh tomatoes, peeled (p. 45)
6 tablespoons tomato paste
3 tablespoons lemon juice
3 tablespoons water

Lemon Twist Garnish. *Slice a lemon thinly with a sharp knife. Make a small cut into one side of the slice and twist outwards.*

Pat the fish dry with paper towels, season the cavities with salt and pepper and tuck two lemon slices into each fish.

Melt 60 g/2 oz/¼ cup of the butter in a large roasting pan. Roll each snapper in the butter to coat both sides. Bake in a preheated oven at 180°C/350°F/gas 4 for 20 minutes or until cooked (p. 23). Lift the fish on to a heated platter and keep warm.

Melt the remaining butter in a saucepan, add the remaining ingredients and stir until combined, breaking up the tomatoes with the edge of a spoon. Simmer for 5 minutes and spoon the sauce over the snapper.

Serves 4

Tarragon Fish Gratin

If fresh tarragon is not available, use half the quantity of dried or substitute dill, another excellent herb used frequently when cooking fish.

4 x 200 g/7 oz firm white fish fillets	*200 ml/7 fl oz/3/4 cup single (light) cream*
Salt and pepper	*1 tablespoon chopped tarragon*
150 ml/1/4 pint/2/3 cup white wine	*4 tablespoons fresh breadcrumbs (p. 17)*
1 sprig of tarragon	*60 g/2 oz/¼ cup butter, melted*
30 g/1 oz/2 tablespoons butter	*Creamed potatoes, to serve*
30 g/1 oz/2 tablespoons plain (all-purpose) flour	*Steamed vegetables, to serve*

Place the fish fillets in a greased baking dish. Season with salt and pepper. Pour over the wine and add the sprig of tarragon. Cover with foil and bake in a preheated oven at 180°C/350°F/gas 4 for about 10 minutes.

Melt the butter in a saucepan, add the flour to make a roux (p. 48). Cook for about 2 minutes, stirring continuously, then set aside to cool. Heat the cream, simmer for 3 minutes until it thickens slightly. Whisk or stir the hot cream into the roux until the sauce combines. Set aside.

Remove the fish from the oven. Pour the pan juices into another saucepan and boil to reduce by half. Add slowly to the cream sauce over a moderate heat, whisking or stirring continuously until sauce boils. Add the chopped tarragon.

Pour the sauce over the fish, sprinkle with the breadcrumbs and melted butter and grill (broil) or return to the oven until golden brown.

Serve with creamed potatoes and a colourful combination of steamed seasonal vegetables.

Serves 4

Above: Preparation of Baked Trout with Lemon Cream Sauce. Add the cooking juices to cream and lemon juice for this wonderful sauce. Left: This is a simply delicious dish which can be adapted to larger or smaller fish varieties.

Baked Trout with Lemon Cream Sauce

This simple dish can be adapted to the size of the fish you're able to get. Alter the quantities and adjust the baking time if necessary.

1 x 800 g/1¾ lb (or 2 x 375 g/12 oz) whole salmon trout
250 ml/8 fl oz/1 cup white wine
125 g/4 oz/1/2 cup butter, melted
Salt and pepper

3 spring onions (scallions), cut into 7.5 cm/3 inch lengths, blanched (p. 31)
2 carrots, cut into julienne strips, blanched (p. 31)
3 tablespoons single (light) cream
1–2 tablespoons lemon juice

Place the fish in a large baking dish, pour over the white wine and melted butter. Season with salt and pepper.

Place the spring onions and carrot on top of the fish, cover with foil and bake in a preheated oven at 230°C/450°F/gas 8 for 15–20 minutes or until cooked (p. 23). Remove from the oven and keep warm while you make the sauce.

Pour the cooking juices from the fish into a saucepan and boil to reduce slightly. Add the cream and lemon juice and reduce until it has thickened. Serve with the trout.
Serves 4

Pine Nut-Crumb Baked Mackerel

A Sicilian-style crumb crust incorporating pine nuts and raisins and the citrus flavour of orange. It's perfect with any oily type of fish.

4 x 250 g/9 oz mackerel, cleaned
Salt and pepper
5 tablespoons fresh breadcrumbs (p. 17)
2 oranges

125 g/4 oz/1 cup raisins, soaked in water for
   about 10 minutes
125 g/4 oz/1/2 cup pine nuts
6 tablespoons virgin olive oil

Season the mackerel with salt and pepper. Arrange in a greased casserole dish.

Mix the breadcrumbs with the grated peel of 1 orange, the raisins and pine nuts. Squeeze the juice from the orange and pour 3 tablespoons over the mackerel. Pour over the olive oil and cover with the breadcrumb mixture. Bake in a preheated oven at 200°C/400°F/gas 8 for 20–25 minutes. Remove from the oven. Cut the remaining orange into thin slices to garnish the mackerel and serve.

Serves 6

Baked Fish in Filo

This is a simple oven-baked surprise. Filo pastry layers are wrapped around whiting or other similar fillets. The pastry not only protects but provides moisture and flavour to the fish.

8 sheets filo pastry
90 g/3 oz/6 tablespoons butter, melted
4 x 150–200 g/5–7 oz firm white long fish fillets,
   cut in half horizontally
2 tablespoons lemon juice

30 g/1 oz/2 tablespoons butter, extra
8 spring onions (scallions), finely chopped
125 g/4 oz mushrooms, finely chopped
Lemon twists (p. 37) and parsley, to garnish

Brush two sheets of filo pastry lightly with the melted butter. Place one on top of the other. Place two fish fillets in the centre of the pastry square and sprinkle with lemon juice. Repeat for the remaining fillets.

Melt the extra butter in a frying pan (skillet) and fry the spring onions and mushrooms over a moderate heat for 5 minutes. Spoon over the fish fillets and fold the pastry into an envelope enclosing the fish fillets. Place on a greased baking sheet and brush with melted butter. Bake in the upper half of a preheated oven at 200°C/400°F/gas 6 for 15 minutes or until pastry is golden brown. Garnish with lemon and the parsley and serve with seasonal vegetables or tossed salad.

Serves 4

Basque Fish Pie (p. 43). This delectable Spanish-style pie can be devoured hot or cold at a picnic or on the patio.

How To Bake Pastry Blind. *Line a pan as directed in the recipe. Place a piece of lightly greased foil on top of the pastry (shiny side down). Top the covered pastry case with rice or pasta as a weight. Bake in a preheated oven at 200°C/400°F/gas 6 for about 10 minutes. Remove foil and rice or pasta, reduce the temperature to 180°C/350°F/gas 4, prick the base lightly with a fork and continue baking for another 15 minutes or until the pastry is lightly browned and crisp. Use as required. This is done to firm the base up before adding a pie filling, which may be heavy and interfere with the cooking of the pastry.*

Preparation of Basque Fish Pie. When the fish is added to the pan, cover, reduce the heat and cook until the fish is opaque.

Basque Fish Pie

A pie baked in a fluted flan tin (pie pan) produces a fish, pepper and potato combination,.

500 g/18 oz shortcrust pastry (basic pie dough)

2 tablespoons olive oil

1 large brown onion, thinly sliced

575 g/11/4 lb green pepper (capsicum, bell
    pepper), cut into julienne strips

2 garlic cloves, crushed

1 kg/21/4 lb tuna or firm white fish fillets, cut
    into large dice

1 kg/21/4 lb potatoes, cut into dice

1 litre/13/4 pints/41/4 cups water

3 tablespoons tomato paste

1/2 teaspoon paprika

Salt and pepper

2 tablespoons roughly chopped parsley

1 egg yolk

2 tablespoons milk

Lemon wedges, to serve

Roll out two-thirds of the pastry and line a deep 25 cm/10 inch flan tin (pie pan) with a removable base. Trim the edges and bake blind (left) in a preheated oven at 220°C/425°F/gas 7 for 10 minutes. Remove from oven. Reduce the oven temperature to 190°C/375°F/gas 5.

Heat the oil in a large saucepan, add the onion, peppers and garlic. Fry for 4–5 minutes or until the vegetables soften. Add the fish, cover, reduce the heat to low and cook for 5–6 minutes or until opaque.

Meanwhile, place the diced potato in a large saucepan and cover with the water. Bring to the boil and simmer for 15 minutes. Drain the potato and add to the fish mixture. Add the paprika, salt, pepper, parsley and tomato paste, with a little water if the mixture seems dry. Spoon into the baked pie shell.

Roll the remaining pastry and any trimmings out into a circle. Place on top of the pie, and trim the edges. Brush with the combined egg yolk and milk. Place in the oven and bake for 20–25 minutes or until the pastry is golden. Leave to stand for 5 minutes and then cut into wedges. Serve with lemon wedges and salad.

Serves 6

Making a Fish Pie

Line a fluted flan tin (pie pan) with half the pastry.

Cook vegetables in a pan, then cook fish fillets until just opaque.

Put potatoes, tomato paste, seasonings, fish and vegetables in pie.

Cover with pastry, trim and brush with eggwash.

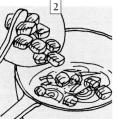

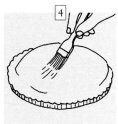

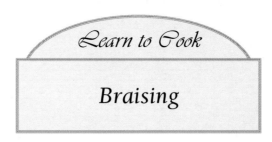

Braising

When braising fish, the time involved must be minimal or overcooking will result in fish that is crumbly and dry. Spices or flavourings are pan-fried first, liquid is usually added and the fish is tossed in towards the end of the cooking time. The liquid used is maintained at a simmer. Liquid that boils rapidly over a period will break up and overcook the fish. The method of layering the potatoes in the following Boullinada recipe gives more than interest to the dish—it acts as a protective barrier too.

Boullinada

This is a Spanish version of a Bouillabaisse and is a hearty fish stew you can prepare easily.

1 teaspoon butter	Salt and pepper
4 garlic cloves, crushed	1 kg/2 1/4 lb potatoes, thinly sliced
200 g/7 oz red pepper (capsicum, bell pepper),	800 g/1 3/4 lb firm white fish fillets
cut into julienne strips	1 litre/1 3/4 pints/4 1/4 cups water
2 onions, coarsely chopped	2 tablespoons olive oil
1-2 red chillies, seeds removed, sliced	Garlic bread, to serve (p. 44)
1 cup chopped parsley	

Melt the butter in a large saucepan, add the garlic, red peppers, onions, chillies and parsley. Season with salt and pepper. Cook for about 5 minutes, stirring continuously until the onions soften.

Layer half the potato slices on top of the parsley mixture, followed by half the fish, more potatoes, the remaining fish and potatoes. Pour in the water, cover and bring to the boil, over a high heat. Add the oil and cook rapidly for 15 minutes to reduce the liquid and thicken the sauce. Serve with garlic bread.

Serves 4

Garlic Bread. *Cut a small loaf of French or Italian bread into fairly thick slices, cutting all the way through. Spread the cut surfaces with garlic butter (see recipe above). Re-assemble the loaf and wrap it in foil. Bake in a preheated oven at 190°C/375°F/gas 5 for 20 minutes, open foil and bake a further 5 minutes, or until crunchy. Serve immediately.*

Preparation of Spicy Fish Curry. Here's an important hint—always cook ground spices to release their aromatic flavour.

Spicy Fish Curry

You can add some coconut cream or plain yoghurt as a variation and serve with crisp poppadums and fruit chutney.

675 g/1½ lb firm white fish fillets
2 tablespoons oil
2 onions, sliced
12 mm/½ inch piece fresh root ginger, grated
2 garlic cloves, crushed
1 teaspoon turmeric
½ teaspoon chilli powder

A pinch each of ground coriander, cloves, cumin,
   cardamom, paprika and cinnamon
3 tomatoes, peeled (below), chopped
Grated peel of 1 lemon
125 ml/4 fl oz/½ cup water
Cooked rice, to serve

Peeling Tomatoes. *Use ripe tomatoes only! Cut out the core, using a small knife. Plunge into boiling water for 1–2 minutes. The skin will start to lift (assisted if you prick the skin with a fork beforehand). Refresh under cold water, peel off the skin. Use as needed.*

Peeled and Seeded Tomatoes (Concasse). *Cut each peeled tomato in half. Squeeze gently, or scoop out the seeds with a teaspoon. Flatten each half gently and cut into small cubes.*

Spicy Fish Curry (p. 43). Served with rice and tasty curry accompaniments, this Asian dish will leave your taste buds tingling.

Wash the fish fillets and dry with paper towels. Cut into largish serving pieces.

Heat the oil in a heavy-based pan (skillet), add the onions and fry over a low heat for 4–5 minutes or until soft. Add the ginger, garlic and all the spices. Cook for 2 minutes, stirring continuously. Add the tomatoes, lemon peel and water, cover and simmer for 15 minutes.

Add the fish pieces, cover and simmer for a further 10 minutes or until fish is cooked (p. 23). Serve with rice and suggested curry accompaniments.

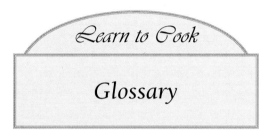

Learn to Cook

Glossary

Batter A mixture of flour and liquid beaten together until it is smooth and at pouring consistency, used to coat food. The addition of egg whites makes it lighter.

Blanch To place vegetables to boiling water for a few seconds and then refresh them under cold water to stop any further cooking. This process brings out their colour and softens them slightly.

Capers Pickled buds of a Mediterranean shrub.

Cardamom Commonly used to flavour rice dishes. The pods are the dried fruits of a plant found in India, related to the ginger family. Available in either seed or ground form.

Cayenne pepper The ground dried pods of a red chilli pepper.

Coriander (cilantro) A very aromatic herb used extensively in curries. It is a member of the parsley family.

Couscous A cereal often used in North Africa. It is processed from semolina into tiny grain-like particles.

Cumin A spice used in Mexican, Indian and Latin American cooking. This ground, dried seed of a plant belonging to the carrot family is highly aromatic.

Curry paste A blend of different spices such as cumin, coriander, ginger, chilli, garlic and turmeric in an oil, such as rapeseed. It comes in different strengths.

Deglaze To add stock or wine to a pan after excess fat has been poured off and to incorporate pan residues into the liquid—usually to make a sauce.

Dice To cut into small even cubes.

Dill A herb from the parsley family. The leaves are used fresh or dried.

Dijon mustard A hot mustard, containing wine, which makes it suitable for use in sauces and dressings.

Filo A pastry with many thin layers of incorporated fat. It is very fragile and dries out quickly, so requires care when handling.

Flake To separate or break into small pieces with a fork.

Ginger Commonly used in Asian cuisine, it is the highly aromatic root stem of a south-east Asian plant.

Goujon. A thin strip of fish or meat.

Julienne strips Even-sized sticks of vegetables or fruit. The thickness depends on the dish and use.

Marinate To let food stand in a marinade to season and tenderize. The marinade usually contains an acid for this purpose as well as other flavourings which penetrate the food immersed in it.

Poppadums Thin wafers, commonly consumed with curries, made from lentil flour, spices and salt. Some contain raising agents and spices.

Paupiette A thin strip of fish or meat rolled around a filling or stuffing.

Pine nuts Small, oval, cream-coloured kernels.

Reduce To boil liquid for the purpose of evaporating some of its water, thus concentrating flavours and consistency.

Reduction The liquid from the process of reducing.

Roux Melted butter and flour which is cooked over a fairly low heat, to which milk, wine or stock is added. This forms the basis of many sauces and soups.

Soured cream A thick, commercially cultured cream.

Soy sauce Used extensively in Asian cooking, made from fermented soya beans.

Tarragon A very aromatic herb, with a slightly tart flavour. Often used to flavour marinades and vinegars. Its flavour complements fish.

Turmeric A bright yellow powder produced from the dried root stem of a plant related to the ginger family. Commonly used in curries.

Vinaigrette A salad dressing based on a combination of oil, vinegar and seasonings.

Whisk To beat at high speed, with a fork or wire whisk, using a circular motion to combine ingredients.